Our American Family™

I Am Korean American

Robert Kim

The Rosen Publishing Group's
PowerKids Press™
New York

To Len—the best friend an author ever had.

Published in 1997 by The Rosen Publishing Group, Inc.
29 East 21st Street, New York, NY 10010

First Edition

Book Design: Erin McKenna

Photo Credits: Cover © Noble Stock/International Stock Photo; background © Icon Comm/FPG International Corp.; p. 4 © Jim Cummins/FPG International Corp.; p. 7 © Travelpix/FPG International Corp.; p. 8 © FPG International Corp.; p. 11 © Popperfoto/Archive Photos; p. 12 © Darlene Hammond/Archive Photos; pp. 15, 16, 20 © Jean Kugler/FPG International Corp.; p. 19 © H. Armstrong Roberts Inc.

Kim, Robert.
    I am Korean American / by Robert Kim.
        p.   cm. — (Our American Family)
    Includes index.
    Summary: A Korean American child talks about aspects of her Korean heritage, including clothing, foods, and customs.
    ISBN 0-8239-5013-1
    1. Korean Americans—Juvenile literature. [1. Korean Americans.]
    I. Title. II. Series.
E184.K6T87 1997
973'.04957—dc21
                                          96-40520
                                          CIP

Manufactured in the United States of America
                                          AC

Contents

The Kwon Family

My name is Nina Kwon. My parents came to the United States from South Korea. My sister, April, and I were born in Baltimore, Maryland. My father works as a high school teacher and my mother is a doctor. My family follows many American and Korean **traditions** (truh-DISH-unz). We are American, but my family believes that it is important to honor our Korean **heritage** (HEHR-ih-tij).

◀ Talking with family members can teach people about their heritage.

5

Korea

Korea used to be one country. Today, it is separated into North Korea and South Korea. My parents and relatives are from South Korea. Seoul is the capital of South Korea. Many families in Seoul live in apartment buildings. Outside the city the homes are different. The doors are often made of rice paper. And the same rooms are sometimes used for different things throughout the day. When my mother was a little girl, her family's dining room turned into her parents' bedroom at night.

Almost one-quarter of South Korea's citizens live in Seoul. ▶

The Korean War

In 1950, North Korea **invaded** (in-VAY-ded) South Korea. The United Nations sent soldiers to help the South Koreans defend their land against the North Koreans. Thousands of soldiers from the United States and other countries fought with the South Koreans. Many people suffered and died during this war. Many Koreans lost friends and family members.

The Korean War lasted for three years. In 1953, North and South Korea reached a **cease-fire** (SEES-fyr). The two parts of Korea officially became two separate nations.

◀ Soldiers in Korea dug trenches to protect themselves during the Korean War.

Dr. Sammy Lee

Sammy Lee is a Korean American whom I admire. He was born in California, but his parents came from Korea. When Sammy was young, he loved swimming and diving. When he got older, he studied medicine. But Sammy never forgot his love for diving. In 1948, he dove in the Olympic Games in London and won a gold medal. He also dove in the 1952 Olympics in Helsinki, and won a bronze medal.

Later, Sammy became a surgeon in California. He also started a swimming and diving school. Sammy Lee is a successful Korean American.

America was very proud when Sammy won his medal in 1948.

Margaret Cho

Margaret Cho was born in San Francisco in 1968. While Margaret was growing up, Korean traditions were very important in her family. Margaret became interested in theater and acting when she was young. Later, in college, she learned there weren't a lot of roles for Asian actors. So she tried stand-up comedy instead. After a lot of hard work, Margaret was doing her stand-up **routine** (roo-TEEN) on TV. Today, she is a successful actress and comedian. Maybe I'll be famous too someday!

◄ Margaret often uses her experiences growing up in a Korean American home in her comedy.

Han-bok

Han-bok (HAHN-book) is the traditional Korean clothing that my family wears on special occasions. These clothes are a lot like those my **ancestors** (AN-ses-terz) wore long ago. My father wears wide pants gathered at the ankles and a long jacket that ties on the side. He also wears a small black hat with a wide brim. My mom, my sister, and I wear short tops with long sleeves and long skirts. We wear *han-bok* for birthdays, weddings, and on New Year's Day.

Wearing *han-bok* reminds Korean Americans of their heritage. ▶

New Year's Day

One holiday that my family celebrates is Korean New Year's Day. On January 1, my family gets up very early and everyone dresses in *han-bok*. First, we have a **ceremony** (SER-eh-mohn-ee) to honor our relatives who have died. Then we have a huge meal with lots of delicious Korean food. After eating, we play traditional games. My favorite game is called *Yut*. It is a board game played with special sticks. I like to play it with my sister and my cousins.

◀ Many Koreans honor their country on New Year's Day.

17

Food

When we have guests for dinner, my mom makes **kim-chee** (KEEM-chee). *Kim-chee* is made with pickled cabbage, different vegetables, and hot peppers. She also serves rice, which we usually have with every meal. Rice is scooped up with small squares of roasted seaweed, called *kim*. Mom also makes **pah-jen** (PAH-jin), which is made of spinach, bean sprouts, and a vegetable pancake. We usually use chopsticks when we have Korean dishes, but sometimes it's easier for me to use a fork!

Korean food is a mixture of many different ingredients and flavors. ▶

Birthdays

Korean Americans have a special celebration for a child's first birthday. In the past, when life was hard in Korea, many babies died before their first birthday. So when babies reach their first birthday, it is celebrated with a big family party. I have seen pictures of the party my family had for me when I turned one year old.

Another important birthday is the sixtieth. When someone turns 60, the person is honored with a celebration called *hwan-gap* (WAN-gap).

◀ In Korean culture, older people are treated with much respect.

I Am Korean American

I like being Korean American. I take part in American celebrations, such as Thanksgiving and the Fourth of July. But I also take part in Korean celebrations such as *hwan-gap*.

I enjoy teaching my friends about my Korean heritage. They like to come to my house and eat Korean food. Sometimes I even let them try on my *han-bok*!

I am very lucky to be able to enjoy and learn from two different cultures.

Glossary

ancestor (AN-ses-ter) A member of your family who lived before you.

cease-fire (SEES-fyr) An agreement made during a war to stop fighting.

ceremony (SER-eh-mohn-ee) A special act or series of acts that are done on certain occasions.

han-bok (HAHN-book) Traditional Korean clothing.

heritage (HEHR-ih-tij) The cultural traditions that are handed down from parent to child.

hwan-gap (WAN-gap) A celebration for a person who turns 60.

invade (in-VAYD) To attack and try to take control of another place.

kim-chee (KEEM-chee) A Korean dish made with pickled cabbage, assorted vegetables, and hot peppers.

pah-jen (PAH-jin) A Korean dish made with spinach, bean sprouts, and a vegetable pancake.

routine (roo-TEEN) The jokes and stories that make up a comedian's act.

tradition (truh-DISH-un) The customs, beliefs, and religions that are passed down from parent to child.

23

Index